HYPNOTIC BS

Belief System Modification Through Self-Hypnosis

Ron Anger

RedCrowHypnosis.com

Copyright © 2024 Ron Anger

ISBN: 979-8-9918849-0-7

All Rights Reserved.

All rights reserved. No part of this publication may be reproduced, distributed, or transmitted in any form or by any means, including photocopying, recording, or other electronic or mechanical methods, without the prior written permission from the author, except in the case of brief quotations embodied in critical reviews and certain other noncommercial uses permitted by copyright law.

Ron Anger
Red Crow Hypnosis
130 S. Red Oak Way
Temple, GA 30179

www.RedCrowHypnosis.com

Ron Anger hosts in-person and online group hypnosis sessions. More information is available at: RedCrowHypnosis.com/events

Table of Contents

Why Read This Book 1

Chapter 1: Deciding to Change Your BS 5

Chapter 2: Your Belief System Can Hold You Back ... 15

Chapter 3: The Process 27

Chapter 4: What Are Core Beliefs? 35

Chapter 5: What Is Hypnosis? 41

Chapter 6: Addressing the Thought, Emotion, Action Cycle 47

Chapter 7: Acknowledging the Belief 53

Chapter 8: Breaking the T-E-A Cycle 59

Chapter 9: PN4 Breathing Practice 67

Chapter 10: Mindfulness 75

Chapter 11: Words Matter—Affirmations 81

Chapter 12: Self Hypnosis 87

Chapter 13: Repetition 97

Chapter 14: A Realistic Timetable 103

Chapter 15: A Final Thought 107

WHY READ THIS BOOK

Have you ever done something or responded to something or someone and then thought *What the hell was that?* Perhaps you felt something that just set you off. A wave of emotion. Whether it was anger or sorrow. But yet, you had no reasonable reason why you responded the way you did.

That reaction was a direct result of your belief system. Somewhere deep inside you is an emotion tied to your reaction. We've all experienced this at some point in our lives. There is no rational explanation. It's a knee-jerk reaction to stimuli.

That reaction becomes an issue when it prevents you from achieving your goals and desires. The most prominent belief in people is the belief that they are not worthy. Not worthy of success. Not worthy of respect. Not worthy of love.

I'm here to call bullshit. You should know that your belief system should work *for* you not against you. By changing what you believe to be true, you change yourself and the world around you. You are capable of change. You are capable of creating the life you desire.

I've been where you stand. I've been guilty of letting the beliefs I held prevent me from success and happiness. I've read the books. I've watched the videos—far too many to count. I've done the self-help path. While the information was helpful and truthful in one way or another, they were all lacking the whole picture.

That's what this book is for. I've written down the information needed to make permanent change—with steps from A to Z. I know that if you follow these steps, you too can make changes to your belief system. You can achieve success. You can achieve happiness. You can achieve love. You can achieve anything you set your mind to. The only thing standing in your way are the beliefs you hold. Think of all the ways your life would be better if you believed in yourself. Think of all the things you could achieve if only you believed you could. That is the starting point to making the life you want. You must believe you can.

This book is a guide to making those changes. It's a map to achieving your goals and desires. It's a blueprint to create the life you want. It's a journey to becoming the best version of yourself.

I am assuming that you are ready to make those changes. You did purchase this book. I am thrilled that you decided to choose my book to guide you on your journey. I can promise you that when you apply what I am teaching, you will not be the same person as when you started this journey.

Just a few things before you start…

- I would strongly suggest that you read this book completely and then go back and reread the chapters and then do the exercises. This will give you an overview of the whole process and then allow you to put it into practice.

- There are a few exercises that would benefit you recording the exercise to play back for yourself when it's time to practice. This is not required but I believe you will benefit more from doing it this way.

- You must decide that you want to change. Yes, this is a decision, a choice. You must want it. State that decision out loud. You will find that once you make the decision to change, it will become easier to take the steps to do so.

"Change your thoughts and you change your world."

—Norman Vincent Peale

Chapter 1

Deciding to Change Your BS

"I will never be good enough..." That thought has gone through everyone's mind at one point or another.

Clive was always anxious and apprehensive when it came to pursuing any of his dreams. From an early age, he was told that he needed to do better, be better. When he spoke of his dreams, Clive was told that he would never be able to support himself. That his dreams were silly. In his daily life, it seemed he could never do anything right. Everything that Clive tried to accomplish would end in disaster. He never seemed to be good enough.

What was Clive's dream? Clive wanted to help people. Plain and simple. He wanted to help people overcome the obstacles that held them back from achieving the success that they dreamed of. He knew the ins and outs of what stops people from becoming who they want to be. He knew what would need to change in order for others to see themselves as everything they were.

What was Clive's problem? He fell into the same rut that the vast majority of people do. He didn't think he was good enough, worthy enough, for people to listen to. Clive suffered from self-doubt and imposter syndrome. That nagging little voice that says, "That's no good," "No one cares what you have to say,'" or "What makes you think you can help anyone?"

Clive's biggest obstacle was his belief system. He tried everything he could get his hands on to help him move past his obstacles. He tried self-help books. He tried audio recordings. He tried meditation. And still no success.

Clive began to see that everything he tried would do what it said it would if he only allowed it. It wasn't the external issues that were causing his problems. It was the internal dialog that he constantly spoke to himself. All of it was WHAT HE BELIEVED TO BE TRUE ABOUT HIMSELF.

Once Clive actually focused his attention on what was creating his problems, it was just a matter of changing the way he viewed himself. Using hypnosis, Clive was able to change the self-defeating belief system that had been installed throughout his life. He was able to replace "I'm not good enough" with "I have something important to share." He changed the "Why would anyone listen to me?" to "I've been there and can help you get out of that rut."

Clive changed his belief that he was unimportant to anyone. That allowed him to see himself as someone who can help others. Clive's belief system was what was holding him back from achieving his dreams. Now that his belief system reflects that he is worthy, that he is important, and that his story has meaning, he is out there sharing what he has learned and changing people's lives.

Everyone wants to be important. Wants to be seen and heard. Wants to feel like their stories matter. The unfortunate truth is most people will never take the time or put in the effort to change. Every day someone's little voice tells them that no one cares. And each time that happens, another brick is laid into the foundation of their belief system. Your belief system dictates your life. If your belief system dictates that you are miserable and unhappy, don't you want to change it? The cost of living with a self-defeating belief system is a life of unfulfilled potential. Think of what you could accomplish if you gave yourself permission to do so.

Hypnosis can be used to change how you think about yourself. That is what this book is all about. I invite you to come along on this journey and change your perceptions of who you are.

Henry Ford stated, **"Whether you think you can or you think you can't—you're right."**

Are your dreams tucked away in an old dusty drawer somewhere? The vast majority of people are held back by their belief system. Changing the way you see yourself will open a floodgate of possibilities. Hypnosis can break down the walls that your beliefs have built.

Imagine for just a moment that all your "No, I can't" cynicisms changed to "Yes, I can." How different would your life be? Or maybe your "I don't matter" to "I have something important to share." What would that do for you?

At this point, you have two choices:

1. You can stay on the path you're on and nothing will change. Your dreams, your self-worth, the life you want for yourself will remain in that drawer… collecting more dust… or

2. You can take the steps necessary to change what you believe to be true about yourself, allowing yourself to become who you want to be.

Your BELIEF SYSTEM is what defines you, and it's time that you believed in yourself. Hypnosis can change the way you see yourself.

In this book, I will share with you how hypnosis can be used to change your belief system and create the you that you've always wanted to be.

Hypnosis is a powerful tool to make changes. It speaks directly to your subconscious mind, bypassing your critical conscious mind. Hypnosis has been used to help athletes overcome limiting beliefs and improve their performance, and it's been successful in helping individuals stop smoking or lose weight. It has helped speakers overcome their fear of speaking in front of large groups. And it can help you change your views on yourself (and, in turn, the way you see the world around you). You can change your beliefs, and you can make your life better!

Gina belonged to a local horticulture club. She enjoyed going to the meetings, but she always sat off to the side in the back of the room. The club had a good number of members from around the local areas. She had been going to the meetings for almost two years now. She knew most of the members and was comfortable chitchatting with them.

But then she was asked to give a talk about growing roses at an upcoming meeting. She panicked! Her mind went straight to "Who am I to tell these people about growing roses?" She dwelled on speaking in front of the group and how many things could go wrong and make her look foolish. She began to think that the other group members would judge her for not knowing much about the rose industry. They would think she was stupid. She even convinced herself that she would be better off not going to any more meetings—that way she wouldn't have to speak.

Gina's close friends had told her many times how beautiful her roses were. They wished they could grow the gorgeous red and yellow flowers that populated her garden. She would always say, "Oh, I just water them and give them a trim; it's nothing special." She would always change the subject because she didn't believe her roses (or herself) were anything extraordinary.

While having tea with a friend (a beautiful bouquet of roses on the table), she told them about the talk that her club wanted her to give. Her friend gushed about Gina's roses. Gina responded with, "I don't know why anyone would want to hear me talk about my hobby." After several minutes of her friend trying to convince her that she did have a green thumb, and that people would be interested in her story, Gina attempted to change the subject again.

Her friend then said, "I don't know why you don't believe in yourself, everyone knows you're the lady to come to for roses."

Gina simply blushed and again tried to change the subject. Her friend then suggested that she make an appointment with the local hypnotist to overcome her fear of speaking. Gina never thought about seeing a hypnotist. After all, how could that possibly help her? But her friend insisted, and Gina finally gave in and made an appointment.

The hypnotist explained to Gina that her fears were based in her belief system: that she believed she was unimportant and that she believed she had nothing to say that anyone wanted to hear. And due to those beliefs, she thought that people would think she didn't know anything and would look foolish.

Gina's hypnotist helped her to get past the limiting beliefs that she had about herself. The sessions allowed Gina to see that she did indeed have a story to share. That people would see her as someone who knew what she was talking about. Gina's beliefs were holding her back. Now that she was able to change her beliefs—with hypnosis—she saw her life in a whole new light.

Gina went on to give an incredible talk about roses and what she did to make them grow. The members of her local horticulture club were so impressed with her talk and her knowledge of roses that they insisted she speak at the state horticulture seminar in the fall. Gina's talk was a huge success.

Thanks to hypnosis and changing her belief system, Gina gives talks about her garden and her roses regularly and never sits in the back of the room anymore.

I am writing this book as a way to help more people. To help you take control of your beliefs and turn them into something positive. I am a certified professional hypnotist. I have worked my way through the issues of my self-defeating beliefs. And I'm here to tell you, once you change your beliefs about yourself, the world becomes a totally new experience. I have been helping people see that they are far more than what they have believed themselves to be.

There are many ways to overcome self-doubt, but I believe that hypnosis is the best way to speak directly to the part of your mind that's responsible for the looping thoughts that we all have. It's a wonderful feeling when you shift from negative thoughts to ones of positive influence. I know if you join me on this journey, by the end you will understand that changing your belief system will change your entire world.

I have worked with several young women who went through terrible ordeals in their childhood that instilled a belief that they weren't good or important. We went to the root of their issues that were causing the looping thoughts of low self-esteem and worthlessness. They were able to see that these thoughts were forced on them by others and had become part of their belief system. They have been able to change their beliefs about not being good enough and move on to a better life.

I've also helped people to change their beliefs about their relationships. They couldn't find or keep a personal relationship because they believed they weren't worthy of love. Once we identified the repeating loop, we changed it to a positive one, and they began to see why certain types of individuals were coming into their lives. Now that their beliefs about being worthy of love have changed, they will never accept anything less again.

I know if you follow along and take action on the ideas in this book, you, too, can change your beliefs about yourself. Imagine for a moment how different your life would be if...

a) your self-esteem was high

b) your self-worth was positive

c) you believed in yourself

Hypnosis can help make ALL these things possible. Imagine if you woke up tomorrow morning ready for the day instead of dreading it. By following along in this book and taking the action necessary, I know your tomorrow will be bright and full of unlimited potential. That being said, YOU must be ready to make the changes to make a better tomorrow. Hypnosis is not a magical pill that will simply make things happen. YOU have to want to change. Changing your belief system with hypnosis is easy if you are ready and willing.

Changing your belief system using hypnosis will allow you to change your views of yourself and ultimately the world around you. If you are ready to make those changes, keep reading. Together we can take those negative looping thoughts and turn them into something positive. We can make you see that all those negative, self-limiting, disabling beliefs you have are an old story. It's time to write a new story. One that is worthy of YOU!

"Valor grows by daring, fear by holding back."

—Publilius Syrus

Chapter 2

Your Belief System Can Hold You Back

I personally became interested in belief systems many, many years ago. I read all the books, watched video tutorials, and listened to speakers. And, in my brain, I knew exactly what I should do. However, like most of us, knowing what to do and doing what we should do are two completely different things. It's easy to have the knowledge and to say, "I'll do it tomorrow," "I'll start in the morning," or "I'll do it right after I finish this other task."

Since I was young, I have been under the belief that no matter how good I was at anything I did, people wouldn't be interested in what I had to share. I've been drawing, painting, and sculpting from a very early age and, deep down, I knew that my artwork was very good, very direct, and aesthetically pleasing. However, I also remembered from a very early age that I shied away from showing people because I didn't want them to tell me the work was no good.

The belief system that I had in place was holding me back. It prevented me from seeing the potential I had to touch a lot of people's lives. My beliefs about my artwork came from within me. All my life I've been told by people close to me that my art was incredible and that I should pursue it. So somewhere along the line, I planted it in my own head that people wouldn't be interested in what I had to show them. I missed many opportunities due to the belief that my work was not something other people would want to see.

Why am I telling you all this? It's really quite simple; most people realize what it takes to make a change. The vast majority of people know that in order to get where they want to be, it requires them to make changes and boldly step forward. Having the knowledge to make those changes and taking the steps to accomplish those changes are two very different animals. It's easy for your mind to wrap around the knowledge of what needs to be done. But we tend to make things more difficult than they need to be. The truth is that 99.5 percent of the time the obstacle that is in our way is ourselves.

When our belief system doesn't match up with what we envision for ourselves, it creates stagnation. We are all adept at wallowing in the mud that we create for ourselves. Our minds concoct all manner of excuses to keep us in one place. That's not a good thing or a bad thing; it's just our mind looking to the past to foretell the future. If something is uncomfortable, our mind looks for ways to avoid it. Unfortunately, when the little voice in our head repeats things over and over and over again, it becomes what we believe. It becomes our belief system.

A lot of people, myself included, have negative belief systems about themselves. I want you to think about this for a moment. Do you speak to yourself the way that you speak to your friends? Typically, we lift our friends up. If they're going through a tough time, we tell them it'll all be all right. If they're doubting themselves, we tell them how wonderful they are. But how many times do you look at yourself and give yourself the same advice? Think about how different your life would be if you simply changed what you believed to be true about yourself.

The solution to these problems is blatantly obvious. It's staring us squarely in the face. If you don't change what you believe about yourself, the way you think about yourself, nothing else in your life is going to change.

Here are some examples. Do any of these ring true with you? Has your little voice whispered them into your ear?

> "I'm no good."
> "I'll never amount to anything."
> "No matter what I do, it's never enough."
> "No one cares what I have to say."
> "I will never reach my goals."
> "Nothing works out, so why bother?"
> "Why waste my time? No one cares."

I can just about guarantee that at some point in your life, you've said something along the lines of one of these examples. We've all told ourselves that nobody cares what we have to say. We've all had moments where we've convinced ourselves that our goals are out of reach so why should we try?

Some of these beliefs we've imposed on ourselves. Others have been imposed on us by outside forces—parents, siblings, and even our friends. And then, of course, you have the media, which tells us on a daily loop that the way we look, the way we see the world, the way we act, and the way we talk can all be better if only we buy this newest product. At some point, our brains processed this information and decided it was true. And it was slowly worked into our belief system. If you say your beliefs out loud, you know they're not true. But after repetition, it slowly works its way into our beliefs. And our beliefs become our reality.

Have you ever told yourself that your opinion isn't important? Or maybe no one wants to hear your story? Or maybe you've been in a crowd of people that were talking and you remained silent because you figured no one wanted to hear what you had to say? All these questions come down to a belief that your voice doesn't matter to anyone. But think for a moment. What if someone did need to hear your opinion? What if you were the reason that someone changed their mind and possibly their life? How different would things look then?

Do you believe that nothing ever works out? And if it never works out, why bother to try? What if I told you that was a common belief? Many people believe that no matter what they do, they will never achieve their dreams. So they go to a job that doesn't fulfill them, or worse, one that they hate. They shuffle through life, wishing that something would change. They never put forth the effort because their belief system tells them it's a waste of time.

If you think about it logically, you have all the answers to rectify the issues. So why haven't you done it? That's actually quite simple; having the knowledge to do something is not the same as having the process to do it.

What are the consequences of not changing your belief system? Well, the biggest one would be that your life doesn't change. Are you happy with your life at the moment? Since you're reading this book, I would have to believe that the answer to that is no. And if you're not happy with your life, what's it going to take for you to do something about it?

You can sit back and not do anything, and three months from now, six months from now, a year from now, your life will still be the same. You will still be unhappy. You will still be unfulfilled. You will still be miserable. Is that what you want? I don't believe it is.

If you don't speak up, no one will ever hear the story that you have to share. And what if your story changes someone's perception? If you don't put the effort forth, you will never achieve your goals. What if your goals are within reach? If you don't try, nothing will change. What if your efforts take you further than you could ever have imagined? Sounds like a lot of what-ifs, doesn't it? What if you change your belief system? What if you change the narrative that is on repeat in your head? What if you believed in yourself? Really think about that for a moment. How different would your life be?

I've always been the person who was in the back of the room—listening to what people had to say, taking in all the opinions and suggestions of other people. I never voiced my opinions because, after all, *who am I for anyone to listen to?* Why would anyone care what I had to say? That was all due to the belief system that I had in place. The belief that my voice was unimportant.

It took me a long time to get that belief out of my head and to change it to a belief that what I had to say could help other people. There was a time when I was filling in for a friend who was good at giving advice and really good at helping others see what was right in front of them. When I first stepped into that position, I felt like a fraud. The thought that was running through my head was, *Why would any of these people care what I had to say?*

There was a point during the day when a young woman came in and was distraught about things going on in her personal life. We talked for a few minutes, and I put her at ease, and, just as importantly, she put me at ease. The conversation flowed back and forth, and when it came to an end, she looked at me and said, "Thank you for your advice. I didn't think anybody else out there knew how I felt."

It was at this point that I realized my voice did matter. After that conversation with that young lady, the rest of the day simply flew by, and I helped a lot of people get what they needed and get out of their heads.

The following weekend, I got a call from my friend asking me to go back in and help them out again. I thought the reason they were asking me to fill in again was they needed someone to replace them. However, when I got there, I discovered they'd asked me to go in again because people were asking for me—specifically for me. It was at this moment that I realized that I did have something to say, that I was good at helping people, and that I could relate to others and help them on their way.

It took someone else to point out to me that my opinion was valid in order to change my beliefs. This was the first step—one of many—to making changes to my belief system. I had to reevaluate the way I looked at the world. I had to look at my beliefs and break them down one at a time in order to realize that they weren't serving my best interests. It was not an easy transformation. And that was due to the fact that I had no one to point me in the right direction.

Do you have these obstacles? Perhaps you're afraid to give your opinion because no one will think it's valid. Or maybe you're afraid that someone will think your ideas are silly. Could it be that you're afraid that you'll get shot down and burn in flames?

All these obstacles come from one thing—your **belief system**.

Have you come face-to-face with these obstacles? Have you been doing well and suddenly found yourself thinking that no one would listen? Or perhaps you were all excited about something you were working on or something you were doing that made you feel good, and then those nagging little thoughts got in the way.

Those nagging little thoughts that you're experiencing come directly from your belief system. What you think and how you think about yourself controls and dictates everything you do in your life. It's the reason that when you look at someone who is successful, you become overwhelmed with feelings of inadequacy. Your belief system is also the reason that when you think about your dreams and your goals in your life, you stop short of doing what's necessary to make those dreams and goals a reality.

Take a moment and think about how different your life would be if your belief system uplifted you. Think about how easy it would be to reach your goals. Your dreams would no longer be out of reach.

Our belief systems have a funny little way of convincing us that we are the only one that has this issue. Our beliefs make us think that no one else has the problems we have. Our beliefs make us feel that we can't share what we're going through with anyone else because no one else would understand. Our beliefs can back us into a corner, make us feel like everyone's out to get us, or just simply feel that nothing is worth doing.

But I assure you that you are not alone. Everyone, at some point or another, has felt like their life has no meaning. Everyone suffers from self-doubt at some point in their life.

- It's estimated that roughly 85 percent of people worldwide (adults and adolescents) have low self-esteem.

- Self-doubt can cause individuals to accept stagnation in their careers, forgoing new responsibilities or opportunities that could lead to promotions.

- 80 percent of women and 73 percent of men feel like they're not enough.[1]

- About 41.6 percent of college students have reported feeling overwhelming anxiety in the past year.[2]

---

[1] Ogar, K. "Am I good enough?" *Infinite Health and Wellness*. Accessed September 14, 2024.
https://kathleenogar.com/did-you-know-that-80-percent-of-women-and-73-of-men-feel-like-theyre-not-enough/

[2] Kesherim, R. "Alarming college student stress statistics." *Total Care Therapy*, March 5, 2024.
https://www.totalcareaba.com/statistics/student-stress-statistics

- A lack of confidence can lead to reluctance to seek further education, causing major monetary losses over time.

As you can see, the statistics show that we've all had these feelings.

And you, dear reader, can overcome these feelings of self-doubt and worthlessness. All you need to do is just change your beliefs. Sounds super simple, doesn't it? Well, I guess if it were that easy, none of us would have these feelings, and you wouldn't be reading this book.

You can change your belief system. It's going to require you to want to change your beliefs. It's also going to require a bit of patience, a bit of repetition, and the knowledge that your life will change.

I know you can do this. I have all the faith in the world in you. How do I know you can do this? Because I've stood where you now stand. That first step is always the hardest. I'm guessing that you are ready to change your beliefs and look at the world with fresh eyes. Or you wouldn't be reading this book.

I encourage you to go through this book with an open mind. To learn and apply something new to your life. To make the changes you desire a reality. I encourage you to go forth and be unstoppable.

"Life is a lively process of becoming."

—Douglas MacArthur

Chapter 3

The Process

Feeling overwhelmed now? Like there's no hope left? Well, let me assure you there are ways to change your belief system—to make changes to your core beliefs and improve your life.

The global self-help market (or self-improvement market) in 2023 is estimated to be worth 41.2 billion dollars (USD). It's on track to reach 81.6 billion dollars by the year 2032. As you can see, there are a lot of folks out there trying to improve their lives.

I think the issue with most of the self-help or self-improvement that's on the market now is in the execution of achieving your goals. As I stated earlier, it's really easy to look at something and say that's the problem, but it's quite a different story trying to fix the problem without a specific roadmap. Most people can see what the issue is, whether it's self-esteem or lack of concentration, it's usually very clear. But when it comes to changing those beliefs, most people have no clue where to start.

The other part of the equation is consistency. Many people fail at making the changes they desire because they don't stick with the process. And yes, changing your belief system is a process. Just like anything else in life, you have to be dedicated to making the changes needed.

You are the key ingredient in this recipe. You have to make the decision when the direction of your life needs to be changed. And you have to be willing and dedicated to make those changes.

At this point, I'm going to assume that you are ready to make the changes that you desire in your life. Otherwise, you wouldn't be reading this book. If you're ready to change your life for the better, I invite and encourage you to continue reading.

Core beliefs, formed in early childhood and influenced by external sources, shape our views of ourselves and the world. Hypnosis, by accessing the subconscious, can alter beliefs and behaviors. Changing your beliefs will change how you perceive yourself and everything in your world.

Breathwork, mindfulness, affirmations, and self-hypnosis serve as tools for self-awareness and positive change. Repetition of these practices is key to reshaping belief systems and achieving lasting transformation.

What is a core belief?

Your belief system is made up of your core beliefs. The majority of your core beliefs are formed when you're very young. As you get older, some beliefs are picked up from friends or the media.

A core belief is one that forms your view of yourself and the world around you. Core beliefs can be positive or negative.

What is hypnosis?

Hypnosis is a way to bypass your conscious mind. Your conscious mind is typically critical, analytical, and focused on facts. When using hypnosis to change beliefs or actions, it's important to get to your subconscious mind. Hypnosis allows you to speak directly to your subconscious mind which deals with feelings and emotions.

Addressing the thought/emotion/action process that creates beliefs

Your beliefs are created through a process. That process follows the thought/emotion/action cycle. This cycle has created your core beliefs. This cycle also creates new beliefs that you pick up throughout your life.

Once you clearly understand how your beliefs are created, you can begin to change them using the same process. This process can be used to change your current beliefs or even create new ones that will benefit you.

Acknowledging the belief

The first step in changing any belief is to acknowledge it. Once you acknowledge that the belief is not serving you, you will begin to see how the cycle was created.

Acknowledging that the belief is negative is a powerful beginning. Once you pinpoint the negative belief, it becomes a powerful shift in your mind. From this point, you can begin to craft a new belief to overwrite the old one.

Breaking the T. E. A. cycle

Breaking the thought/emotion/action cycle becomes much simpler once you've acknowledged that the belief is not serving you. Your beliefs all start with a thought, which leads to an emotion and, in turn, an action.

Knowing the thought that has created the belief can allow you to change the emotion attached to it and thereby the action as well.

PN4 breathwork practice

Breathing exercises are a powerful and easy way to focus on the moment. Breathwork signals to the body to relax and release. It's an important beginning to working through belief changes. Once you've learned breathwork, it will be easier to relax and allow your subconscious to be accessed.

Mindfulness practice

Mindfulness is a way to be present in the moment. It allows you to be aware of your thoughts, feelings, and surroundings.

Mindfulness teaches us how to be in the moment and not concerned with the stress of the past or the anxiety of the future.

Affirmations—words matter

Affirmations are simply positive statements that you can say to yourself to shift your mindset and help you achieve your goals. Affirmations can be simple statements. Perhaps only a few words to convey a message or even an acronym that can easily be stated and remembered.

When choosing an affirmation, remember, words matter. Affirmations should be positive and in the present tense.

Mirror practice

Mirror work is simply looking yourself in the eye and lifting yourself up. It's a way of communicating with yourself as if you were a friend. It is a simple way of increasing self-acceptance and reemphasizing the changes you want to make. It can be done at any time of the day.

Bedtime practice

Bedtime practice consists of getting in a meditative state prior to going to sleep and restating your affirmations;

allowing them to comfortably sink into your subconscious mind while you sleep.

It's a simple process and doesn't take a lot of time but yields great dividends.

Self-Hypnosis

Self-hypnosis is easy to do and not time-consuming. It allows you to speak directly to your subconscious mind, giving it the directions that you wish it to follow. On some level, all hypnosis is self-hypnosis. This is due to the fact that you are in control. It is your mind that is making the connections.

Repetition

The secret to getting results—to becoming fluent in doing anything that you set your mind to—is repetition. You have to be willing to repeat the steps in order to get what you want to achieve.

There is, just as in life, no secret shortcut. You have to follow the process to get to the goals you want to obtain. When you do that, you'll be able to change your belief system and change your life.

In the following chapters, you will begin to learn the steps to take in order to change your belief system. We will delve further into the ideas listed above so that you can see the correlation and apply them to making changes.

You will be provided with the knowledge and exercises in order to help you pinpoint the belief that you wish to change and how to do so.

Understanding the impact of core beliefs and the transformative power of practices such as hypnosis, mindfulness, and affirmations gives you the ability to take control of your beliefs and, ultimately, your life.

Through acknowledgment, mindfulness, and the power of repetition, you can reshape your core beliefs, leading to a more enlightened and fulfilling life.

"The next time your core beliefs are challenged – try being curious instead of furious."

—Randy Gage

Chapter 4

What Are Core Beliefs?

Do you know your core beliefs?

Do you know what it is that drives you?

Do you know how your core beliefs came into being?

There are many factors which create your core beliefs. Core beliefs are your ideas of how the world operates, how others operate, and how you see yourself. Core beliefs are typically created when you're young. Through personal experiences or those around you telling you how things work. That could be your parents, your siblings, your culture, or even your social environment.

Core beliefs act as your lens to the world. They can influence emotions, thoughts, and behaviors. Your core beliefs are your foundation and how you see yourself in the world around you. They can affect your self-esteem, your confidence, and how you feel.

Your core beliefs can be positive, negative, or neutral. Positive core beliefs lift you up and give you a sunny disposition, whereas negative core beliefs tend to hold you back or cloud your views of how things are.

Your core beliefs shape your automatic responses and reactions. They operate at a subconscious level. A lot of the time, you may not understand why you reacted the way you did or why you view things the way you do. Core beliefs affect your decision-making, your relationships, and your general overall feelings.

Have you ever felt that the world was unfair? Let's look at that through the following example:

There lived a young woman named Lily who dreamed of becoming a doctor. Lily came from a humble background, where things were always tight, and her family struggled to make ends meet. Throughout Lily's life, she was always told that things couldn't be afforded. However, Lily was determined to pursue her dream of becoming a doctor. She excelled in school, earned scholarships, and worked tirelessly to realize her ambitions.

Despite all her hard work, and caused by unforeseen circumstances, Lily's scholarship was revoked, leaving her with an insurmountable financial burden. Desperate to continue her education, she began looking for financial aid from various sources, but to no avail.

Meanwhile, students from affluent families effortlessly progressed through their studies without having the burden of financial worries.

She became frustrated with the unfairness of the world. Despite her hard work and dedication, it seemed that the odds were stacked against her. She witnessed countless instances of privilege and inequality, further reinforcing her belief that the world was inherently unjust.

The above story illustrates Lily's core belief that money was something she would never have. Even after all her efforts and excelling academically, her dreams were just out of reach again. Those beliefs were reinforced and strengthened by the unfortunate events that took place.

Our story does, however, have a happy ending. Lily realized that her beliefs about money were holding her back and were giving her the perception that the world was unfair.

Despite all the hurdles, Lily refused to abandon her dream. She took on multiple jobs, sought out alternative funding options, and persevered through numerous setbacks. Eventually, Lily managed to overcome the financial obstacles and fulfill her dream of becoming a doctor.

As you can see, core beliefs dictate how we see the world around us. Lily could have easily given up believing that the world was truly unfair, but by shifting her core belief around money, she was able to see alternatives to achieving her goal.

Core beliefs are created by the constant bombardment of information given to our subconscious—in Lily's case, the notion that money was unavailable.

Let's take a look at another core belief:

A young man named Alex had always felt like an outsider. He struggled to fit in and often felt overlooked and unappreciated. This core belief was created when he was a young boy. His parents were both workaholics and never had the time for him. As he entered adulthood, these experiences led Alex to develop a deep-seated belief that he was unworthy of love and affection.

Despite his kind and compassionate nature, Alex found it difficult to form meaningful connections with others. He yearned for love but felt undeserving of it. His belief that he was unlovable became a barrier to forming close relationships, and he often found himself isolated and lonely.

Alex met a kind-hearted woman named Kim. She saw the goodness in Alex and was drawn to his kind demeanor. Despite her efforts to show him love, Alex struggled to accept her affection. He believed that he was inherently flawed and that no one could truly love him.

As their friendship deepened, Kim persisted in showing Alex unwavering support and understanding. Slowly, Alex began to question his long-held belief. He started to see himself through Kim's eyes and realized that he was deserving of love, just like anyone else.

Once he realized that his core belief was incorrect, Alex began to shed the belief that he was unworthy of love. He saw that his self-worth was not defined by his past experiences and that he was capable of giving and receiving love.

Core beliefs can follow you throughout your life, from early childhood into adulthood. They color the way you view yourself. The good news is that core beliefs can be changed.

Are your core beliefs causing your world to be not so rosy? Are they holding you back from achieving what you so desperately desire? Or maybe they're just making things hazy and keeping you from feeling happy?

Now that you have a better idea of core beliefs, I want you to begin to think of any core beliefs that you may have that are holding you back. Sit with this for a few moments and really think about the beliefs that may be causing you to not accomplish your dreams and goals. Take the time to write down any belief that you think may be causing issues for you.

Be honest with yourself and just write down whatever comes to mind. You don't need to justify these beliefs or analyze them. You just need to set them on paper so that when the time comes to deconstruct them, they are there in front of you.

"You use hypnosis not as a cure but as a means of establishing a favorable climate in which to learn."

—Milton H. Erickson

Chapter 5

What Is Hypnosis?

Hypnosis, according to the *Encyclopedia Britannica*, is a "…special psychological state with certain physiological attributes, resembling sleep only superficially and marked by a functioning of the individual at a level of awareness other than the ordinary conscious state. This state is characterized by a degree of increased receptiveness and responsiveness in which inner experiential perceptions are given as much significance as is generally given only to external reality."[3]

Hypnosis is basically the ability to bypass your conscious critical thinking mind. Your conscious mind deals with data and facts. Hypnosis allows you to bypass that and speak directly to your subconscious mind. Your

---

[3] Orne, M. T. & Hammer, A. G. "Hypnosis." *Encyclopedia Britannica*, August 23, 2024. https://www.britannica.com/science/hypnosis

subconscious mind deals with feelings, emotions, and abstract ideas.

Your subconscious mind is where your core beliefs are created and stored. This is why it's difficult to consciously or logically change the way you believe. Trying to change your subconscious beliefs with your conscious mind is like trying to hammer a nail using a screwdriver. It's overwhelming, frustrating, and ultimately useless.

Since your core beliefs are stored in your subconscious, they become automatic responses to things. This can influence thoughts, emotions, and behaviors that do not make any logical sense. Your subconscious beliefs often resist change through conscious efforts. Since they are deeply rooted, it will take more than a logical mindset to overcome them.

Core beliefs are typically emotionally charged. Negative core beliefs are usually overly emotionally charged. The emotions that are attached to the core beliefs make it next to impossible for the conscious mind to fully grasp them. Core beliefs are emotionally anchored thoughts. These thoughts create emotions, which dictate the action you take.

As mentioned above, your core beliefs have a deep influence on your thoughts, emotions, and behaviors, which is why some people can seemingly do the impossible. Their core beliefs deal with their self-esteem in a positive light, whereas negative core beliefs tend to keep people locked in a cycle of self-doubt.

Hypnosis is a fantastic aid in the integration of new, positive core beliefs. Since it bypasses your logical mind, it's easy to introduce new beliefs or change existing beliefs. Hypnosis can allow you to go into your subconscious mind and modify or change the emotion attached to a belief. It's also beneficial in changing the belief itself.

Hypnosis has other benefits, such as stress reduction. It can help you relax and feel calmer. It is also helpful for anxiety as it can help you learn to regulate your emotions and reduce automatic responses. Hypnosis is good for getting rid of bad habits and introducing new, positive habits.

Hypnosis comes in two varieties: hypnotist-led hypnosis or self-hypnosis, but when it comes right down to it, all hypnosis is basically self-hypnosis. That's because, in the end, it's your subconscious that makes the changes. Seeking help from a hypnotist means that somebody else is guiding you. They know the correct words and patterns to get you to where you need to be as quickly as possible. Self-hypnosis, on the other hand, can be audio-led or simply a set of instructions repeated to yourself. Either of the two will lead you to your subconscious mind and allow you to change beliefs and habits.

Self-hypnosis is a wonderful way to make changes. It allows specific criteria and individualized attention to the changes you wish to make. Self-hypnosis is not difficult or overly time-consuming. It just requires a willingness to change and the ability to repeat the process.

Now that you have an understanding of what hypnosis is at a basic level, let's look at some of the issues that people have about using hypnosis:

- Self-hypnosis creates a trancelike state where you lose control.

Hypnosis, whether done in an office with a professional hypnotist or at home using methods of self-hypnosis, allows you to access the subconscious. The trancelike state that is created through hypnosis does not take control away from you. If anything, it allows you more control. It brings more focus and clarity to the situation.

- Self-hypnosis is only for people with certain personality types or mental abilities.

People often assume that it takes a certain type of person to be able to be hypnotized. That simply is not true. Anyone can be hypnotized or use self-hypnosis techniques to improve their lives. An example of this would be when you're watching a movie and your brain wanders; that is a form of the trancelike state that self-hypnosis produces.

Or when you're driving home on a familiar route and you suddenly realize that you're at home, but you don't remember the drive. This is another form of the trancelike state that hypnosis produces. It's something that occurs on a daily basis.

- Self-hypnosis is a one-time event rather than an ongoing practice.

Hypnosis, like meditation or mindfulness practices, is something that can be used on a daily basis. It should be looked at like building a house, one brick at a time. Some people have an easier time using hypnosis than others. I believe the reason for that is due to the fact that they have committed to making changes.

- Self-hypnosis is only effective for specific issues like weight loss or smoking cessation.

Whereas self-hypnosis is an amazing tool for losing weight or stopping smoking, it is also useful for making changes to better your life. Since all these issues are stored away in your subconscious mind, self-hypnosis can help you make the changes to any aspect of your life.

- Self-hypnosis is a mystical or supernatural experience.

Some people think that self-hypnosis is some woo-woo new-age thinking method. That it's not for them because they don't believe in the mystical or supernatural. This thinking comes from your core beliefs. If you're ready to make changes, self-hypnosis can feel mystical or supernatural. But all these feelings are in your subconscious mind. If you allow it to be mystical or supernatural, that's all well and good. However, at the end of it, you will simply find that it's all been enlightening.

"Your thoughts are incredibly powerful. Choose yours wisely."

—Joe Dispenza

Chapter 6

Addressing the Thought, Emotion, Action Cycle

Samantha would constantly worry about the future, dwell on past mistakes, and find the worst in every situation. This, in turn, would lead to feelings of anxiety, depression, and low self-worth. Her negative emotions would then drive her to engage in unhealthy behaviors like overeating, isolating herself, and lashing out at loved ones. It was a vicious cycle that kept her trapped in an unfulfilling life.

There came a point where Samantha realized that if she continued down this path, she would never achieve the happiness and fulfillment she craved. That's when she committed to making a change.

Samantha started by becoming more aware of her thoughts. Whenever a negative thought popped into her mind, she would consciously challenge it. "Is this thought really true?" she would ask herself. "What evidence do I have to support it?"

By questioning her automatic negative thoughts, she was able to start replacing them with more realistic, positive perspectives.

As Samantha's thought patterns improved, she noticed a shift in her emotions as well. Instead of immediately feeling anxious or sad, she found herself experiencing more neutral or even positive feelings in response to life's ups and downs. She no longer let every setback send her into a downward emotional spiral.

She began making an effort to engage in behaviors that supported her newfound positivity, such as exercising regularly, spending time with uplifting friends, and pursuing hobbies that brought her joy. She also worked on setting healthy boundaries and learning to say no to things that drained her energy.

She was no longer paralyzed by fear and self-doubt. Instead, she approached challenges with a sense of resilience and optimism. Her relationships improved as she learned to communicate her needs and show up as her best self.

Samantha finally felt at peace within herself. The dark cloud of negativity that had once consumed her had lifted. She knew that the journey of personal growth was an ongoing one, but she felt empowered and excited to continue making positive changes.

By consciously shifting her thought, emotion, and action cycle, she was able to create the more fulfilling, joyful life she had always wanted. Her transformation serves as an inspiration for anyone seeking to change their negative thoughts and live a more positive life.

Let's take a look now at how your core beliefs are created. A core belief begins with a thought, which typically has an emotion attached to it, and that thought and emotion dictate an action. This is how your core beliefs are created at a basic level.

Keep in mind that whatever thought you have, your brain will look for every opportunity to prove that thought. So, for example, maybe when you were young you thought that dogs were scary and mean. That thought may have been created because your neighbor's dog barked and growled at you every time you walked by. And as you grew up, your brain took every advantage to prove to you that all dogs were mean and scary.

So, from the example, the thought was *Dogs are mean and scary*. The emotions attached to that were fear and mistrust. And the action that the thought and emotion created was avoiding all dogs.

As you can see, your thoughts and emotions can directly influence the actions you take in your daily life. The subconscious mind can create an intricate web of emotions attached to the thoughts that we create. And because of this, you can go through life making decisions without realizing the reasons behind those decisions.

This is the reason people often make self-defeating decisions in their life. Perhaps when you were younger, someone you looked up to made the comment that you would never amount to anything. The emotions that created were self-doubt and hurt. And from that moment, your brain looked for every opportunity to show you that you would never amount to anything. Now you're an adult, and you are still making decisions based on the core belief that you will never amount to anything.

This cycle repeats on an endless loop. Your brain looks for everything that will confirm what you think. If you have negative thoughts, based on the beliefs that you hold, all you will see is proof of those negative thoughts. If you change those core beliefs and replace them with positive thoughts, then your brain will begin to look for confirmations of positive influences.

Your core beliefs are based on past experiences. The beliefs about those experiences create the thought patterns that affect everything you do today. I want you to be aware of this so that going forward, you can begin to see the thoughts and the emotions attached to those thoughts are what drives your actions today.

In order to change your beliefs, you will need to look at the thoughts and the emotions attached to those thoughts. It's a process to work through to get the results you want. The biggest obstacle you'll face is your belief of you being capable of changing. You have to decide if you are ready and committed to making those changes.

"Your chances of success in any undertaking can always be measured by your belief in yourself."

—Robert Collier

Chapter 7

Acknowledging the Belief

The first step in changing your belief system is to acknowledge the belief that you hold. Your belief is the overall package. It consists of the thought, emotion, and action that you take. It's important that you take a hard look at this belief and, above all, you must be honest with yourself.

The drawback to holding on to old beliefs or limiting beliefs is that it prevents you from achieving what you truly desire. Outdated beliefs could be the reason you're unable to be happy or productive or find that perfect relationship. Limiting beliefs could be responsible for you not getting that promotion or making more money. Remember that your belief system is what drives your actions. And your actions are what achieve your goals.

The benefits of examining, challenging, and changing your old core beliefs are manyfold. They may provide you with a way of seeing the world differently. They could help you see that you are worthy of what you desire. They may heal your relationship with money and finances. They could even raise your level of self-love and acceptance. In short, they could simply make you a happier person.

This first step is a hard one. This is when you may get bogged down or simply step into denial. When examining your belief, you must be honest with yourself. This does not mean that you need to be critical of your belief. You must simply acknowledge that the belief exists. And that you are committed to changing it.

The questions you need to ask yourself at this point are:

"What are the beliefs that are holding me back?"

"What are my limiting beliefs?" and

"What beliefs are no longer serving me?"

You must be truthful with yourself. Some of your beliefs could have been created by the people in your life that you love the most. Do not let yourself go down the road of worrying about what others will say. Do not get hung up on the thought that people will not like you. The changes that you seek are yours and yours alone.

Don't be afraid to pull the curtain back and take a peek at what makes the show run. Don't try to analyze any of the beliefs that you come across right now. That will come later. At this moment, you are simply trying to find the reason why.

This is where the work starts to make the changes to better your life. If you are unwilling to be honest with yourself then your changes will not take hold. This will require you to dig deep inside and take a hard look at what propels you. I cannot stress enough that you must be honest with yourself.

Exercise 1: Acknowledging the Belief

I want you to take out a sheet of paper and draw a line across the top, maybe about an inch down, and a line down the center. On the left-hand side at the top, I want you to write Belief. On the right-hand side at the top, I want you to write Emotion.

Now I would like you to find a place to sit comfortably, with no distractions. Turn your cell phone off, turn the radio off, turn the television off, and simply sit in the quiet.

Take a moment and consider the changes you wish to make in your life. Perhaps to improve your self-esteem or focus on your education. Now I would like you to think of the beliefs you have about those changes. Using the examples above, perhaps your issues with self-esteem are: "My parents told me I would never amount to anything." Or perhaps your issues with improving your education come from being told there wasn't enough money to send you to school.

You may get a flood of beliefs about the issue you are addressing. Or you may struggle to come up with just one. These are both normal responses. Whatever you come up with, I want you to write that belief on the left side of your paper. I want you to sit with this for a minute and let the ideas just flow from you.

Now that you have ideas listed about your beliefs, I want you to take a moment and read over them. Then I want you to look honestly at these beliefs and identify the emotion attached to them. Again, you may have many ideas or just one.

I want you to write down the emotion or emotions that are attached to your beliefs on the right-hand side of the paper. Take your time, and again, be honest with yourself. List the emotions that your beliefs are connected with.

If you are struggling to identify the belief or the emotions attached to those beliefs, I want you to do something else. Whether that's taking a walk or vacuuming the floor. Allow your mind to simply focus on something else. Once you take your focus away from the task at hand, you may find that the ideas will simply come to you.

"If you want a new outcome, you will have to break the habit of being yourself, and reinvent a new self."

—Joe Dispenza

Chapter 8

Breaking the T-E-A Cycle

Now that you have your list of beliefs that you feel need to be changed, I want you to pick one. Do not try to do a whole group of them at once. By choosing only one, you are allowing yourself to focus and change the fundamental emotions behind that belief.

Changing the thought, emotion, action cycle is not as difficult as it sounds. I believe this is where most people get hung up. They convince themselves that changing a belief that they've had forever is difficult. And that's why most people fail.

Once you've made the decision that you want to change it, it becomes even easier. That being said, I want you to be aware that it is going to take some work on your part. This is not a *snap your fingers and everything will be different* process. This will require a level of effort and commitment on your part.

Changing the T-E-A cycle consists of defining the thought, focusing on the emotion behind that thought, and then changing the action that is followed by that thought. This is the process of how your beliefs are created. Each belief begins with a thought that is attached to an emotion and followed by an action.

Once you focus on the beliefs that you want to change, it's a simple process to reverse engineer the pattern that created that belief. Some beliefs go deep. Others may be surface dwellers. Be aware that some beliefs are extremely emotional and will require determination and commitment to change.

Let's take a look at an example. I'm going to use one that is related to money, since that is something that everyone can consciously and subconsciously understand.

The belief is "I will never have money."

The thought behind this belief could be any multitude of things. However, for this example, I'm going to use the thought, *Do you think I am made of money?* This is a statement that a lot of people could repeat from their childhood. It's a statement that your parents may have said in your youth.

The emotion behind the thought may be one of *lack* or *disappointment*. It could also be one of *shame* if your friends could afford to have what they wanted. This is not a reflection on you; it is simply a fact from that period in your life. And it is something you can change.

Now that you have the belief, the thought behind that belief, and the emotion of that belief, you can clearly see the actions that follow. You may tell yourself, *I can't afford that*. Or maybe you say, "I shouldn't have it." Or it could manifest in the opposite direction and become *impulse buying* that leaves you in unnecessary debt.

Exercise 2: Writing Your Beliefs

Take a clean piece of paper and draw a line down the center, vertically and horizontally. That will give you four squares.

In the top left-hand corner, I want you to write the belief that you want to change. This will come from the exercise from the previous chapter. Before you write that belief down, I want you to be as concise as you can possibly be with that belief.

In the top right-hand corner, I want you to write down the thought attached to that belief. Don't sugarcoat this or try to make it sound pretty. This is for your eyes only. You may need to think about what it is that makes you believe that.

In the lower left-hand corner, I want you to write down the emotions that you feel when this thought occurs. Again, do not sugarcoat it. You need to be honest with yourself so that you can make honest changes. The emotion attached to this thought could be a single emotion or multiple emotions. Write it all down.

In the lower right-hand corner, I want you to write down the actions that you follow when this belief crops up. You may have to take a moment and truly think about this. Be completely honest with yourself and write down how you react, such as getting mad, crying, or feeling overwhelmed or depressed when this thought and emotion present themselves.

This exercise will become your roadmap of what will be changed in order for you to achieve your goal. If you have been honest with yourself, you will begin to see the T-E-A cycle in process.

Taking the method I gave you, it should look like this:

In the upper left corner, it should say *I will never have enough money*. In the upper right corner, the thought should be *Do I look like I'm made of money?* In the lower left corner, the emotions would say "lack," "disappointment," and "shame." In the lower right corner, the actions would be "Not spending the money" or "Completely overspending."

Now that you have the diagram of your current T-E-A cycle, we will look at creating a new

T-E-A cycle to guide you through making the changes to your beliefs. When creating your new cycle, there is something that you need to be aware of. You must be realistic.

The reason for this is simple: If you have a belief that you are poor, trying to change the belief to "I am incredibly rich" is something that your brain will not process. You must first change the statement to something like "I have enough money." Once you have successfully changed that belief, then you can come back and work on the belief, "I am wealthy."

You must also start to become consciously aware of when your belief kicks in. In the example of money, when you are questioning whether you want to buy something, you must be able to stop yourself and say, "That is my old belief. I am choosing to use my new belief."

Exercise 3: Rewriting Your Beliefs

Take a new, clean piece of paper and draw a line down the center, vertically and horizontally.

The upper left-hand corner is where you're going to write your new belief. Take your belief from the previous exercise and think about how you want to change it. Take a few minutes and actually think about this. State it in the way that you would say it. It doesn't need to be long or fancy. It just needs to be concise and to the point. Saying it out loud may help you verbalize how to write it.

The upper right-hand corner is where you're going to write the thoughts that drive this belief. Think about this and word it how you would say it. Take your time and be honest with yourself.

In the lower left-hand corner, you will write the new emotions that will be attached to your new thought. I want you to think of how you will feel by engaging in your new thoughts. Write these emotions down exactly how you feel them, such as if it will make you happy, you should write "Happy," not "Joyous."

In the lower right-hand corner, you will write down the actions that will follow these new thoughts and emotions. Take a moment and seriously consider what actions you think would come from your new beliefs.

Let's look at the example I gave you previously and how it could be rewritten into a new belief.

In the example, the original belief was "I will never have enough money." We can change that belief to simply say "I always have enough money." It's a simple change that can create a powerful new belief.

The thought behind the original belief was "Do I look like I'm made of money?" The new thought could be written as *That may have been true before, but now I always have enough*, which could further be broken down to *I always have enough money*.

This is a shift in your original thought you will use to stop the old thought from creeping back in. If you feel the old belief coming to the surface, break the thought (and the belief) with, *That may have been true before, but not now. Now this doesn't serve me.*

The emotions attached to the original thought were *lack*, *disappointment*, and *shame*. They could be replaced with *abundance, excitement, and worth*. The stronger the emotion, the more easily the subconscious will accept the new thought.

The actions that followed in the example were about not purchasing anything or purchasing everything. These actions could be changed to taking the time to consider whether or not the purchase has any real meaning, such as *Will this make me happy? Is this something I want, or is this something I need?*

The two exercises in this chapter will help you define a new T-E-A cycle and therefore a new belief. So take your time, be honest with yourself, and as concise as possible. They should also be written in your words. It may be easier to pretend you're having a conversation with a close friend and write down the answers as you would respond to that person.

"Breath is life. We should pay as much attention to it as any other aspect of beingness."

—Swami Nostradamus Virato

Chapter 9

PN4 Breathing Practice

Now that you have your exercises from the previous chapter done, it's time to learn the steps that will help facilitate the changes you wish to make. Remember, this is a process. Each step will build upon the previous one. Taking the time to complete the steps will help you achieve your goals.

In this chapter, we will begin by using breathwork. I'm sure you're asking yourself at this point, "What does breathwork have to do with changing my belief system?"

The short answer to that is breathwork has many benefits that will help you achieve your goals.

Breathwork intentionally changes your breathing pattern, which in turn will improve your mental and physical well-being. Breathwork has been practiced for thousands of years with a multitude of benefits. If you think of yoga, breathwork is one of the fundamentals. It can be simple deep breathing or more advanced techniques. The practice intentionally focuses on the breath, which calms the body and mind.

Some of the many benefits of breathwork include lowering your blood pressure, reducing stress, and improving blood circulation to the body. It can also increase physical energy and improve your immune system.

Breathwork can be used to reduce anxiety and depression. It can help with addictive behaviors and negative thought patterns (such as deep-rooted beliefs). As you can see, breathwork fits in nicely with what you are trying to accomplish.

It also allows for better mental focus with the additional benefit of a much better outlook on life. You will be employing breathwork to increase your mental focus. This will allow you to focus on the positive changes you wish to make.

Breathwork is a simple process that can be used whenever you need it. I would suggest at the start doing it at least twice a day—once in the morning and once in the evening. I'm sure, at this moment, the thought running through your head is *How do I find the time to do that?* And I would ask you, "Are you committed to the changes you want to make?"

The practice shared with you below will take approximately five minutes. Are you willing to spend ten minutes a day in order to change a belief that is no longer benefiting you? Are you committed to making the changes to improve your life? Do you want to be free from the negative thoughts that fill your day?

Then let's begin…

PN4 is a breathing exercise that I've been working on to help replace negative thoughts with positive ones. It's a simple process, does not take long, and will benefit you throughout the processes of changing your belief system.

Exercise 4: Breathing Practice

I want you to find a quiet place where you can get comfortable. You can sit on the floor or in a comfortable chair. Try to keep your back as straight as possible. This will become easier the more you do it.

This is done is a series of three with four deep breaths.

(1)

Now, close your eyes, and take a deep breath in, slowly counting to four.

Hold that breath, counting to four again.

Release that breath, counting to four.

Hold that breath, counting to four.

And again

Take a deep breath in, slowly counting to four.

Hold that breath, counting to four again.

Release that breath, counting to four.

Hold that breath, counting to four.

Repeat two more times.

(2)

Take a deep breath in, and as you slowly count to four, I want you to picture the word POSITIVE and all the good associated with it. Breathe in POSITIVE.

Hold that breath and continue to picture the word POSITIVE, while you count to four again.

Release the breath, and as you count to four, I want you to picture the word NEGATIVE.

I want you to release all the NEGATIVE from your body with your breath.

Hold that breath and count to four, while imagining the NEGATIVE leaving your body.

Repeat three more times.

(3)

Take a deep breath in, and as you slowly count to four, I want you to imagine an image of something POSITIVE and all the good associated with it. Breathe in POSITIVE.

Hold that breath and continue to picture the POSITIVE image, while you count to four again.

Release that breath and, as you count to four, I want you to imagine an image of something NEGATIVE. I want you to feel the NEGATIVE image fade from your body with your breath.

Hold that breath and count to four, while imagining the NEGATIVE image fading from your reality.

Repeat three more times.

Now, I want you to just sit and relax. Breath normally and allow a calm sense of peace to wash over you and fill your entire being. When you're ready, open your eyes, stretch, and know that you are filled with POSITIVE energy.

Congratulations! You have completed the PN4 breathwork. That's it. Wasn't difficult, was it? The whole process should take about five minutes. You are on your way to making your life better and creating the changes you desire. Do this in the morning when you wake up or as close to that as possible. And in the evening just before bed—as an added bonus, you should sleep better as well. This can also be used during the day if things become overwhelming or you feel bogged down.

Just a quick note: To make this easier on yourself, use your cell phone and the record function. You can slowly read through the steps above (count to four in your head) and record it so that you can play it back when doing this exercise. That way you can concentrate on the exercise without having to look at it. Or, if you prefer, you can go to https://redcrowhypnosis.gumroad.com/ and purchase the recording that I have available.

"The present moment is the only time over which we have dominion."

— Thich Nhat Hanh

Chapter 10

Mindfulness

We are now going to begin using mindfulness as the next step in this process. You may have heard about mindfulness, and you may not be sure what that is. Put quite simply, mindfulness is being present in the now—not worrying about the past or stressing over the future but to be in this moment now.

Many people believe that meditation and mindfulness are one and the same. They are not. They can be used together to increase your frequency, your clarity, and your overall well-being.

Mindfulness is being present in the moment without attaching judgment or emotions. It brings your focus to your breathing and the sensations in your body. It's acknowledging the things around you, such as sounds, smells, and sights.

It's not an overly complicated process. But in today's world, where you rush from one moment to the next, it's a needed process. Practicing mindfulness can be as simple as slowing down, listening to the wind rustle through the trees, or hearing the birds sing.

Being mindful has many benefits. It can help to increase your focus and improve your sleep. It will also help to improve emotional regulation and help you feel calmer. Mindfulness is also good for helping to reduce anxiety and depression.

Mindfulness is useful for acknowledging your emotions without becoming entangled in them. That is what we will be using mindfulness for moving forward. In this way, you will be able to view the emotions you have attached to your core beliefs without being overwhelmed by them.

Mindfulness is a practice that can be done at any time throughout your day. It doesn't require a dedicated time or location. It can be done while you're at home, while you're at work, or simply when you're taking a walk.

It only takes a couple of minutes (which can be expanded if needed). And the only requirement is that you take the time to focus on your breathing and notice the things around you.

Mindfulness is particularly useful when you feel emotional, stressed, or overwhelmed. It is something that you can do without anyone else having to know. It can be practiced while you're alone or in a crowded room. Mindfulness can be done while you sit in a packed bus or alone on a park bench.

Now that you have a better understanding of mindfulness, I want you to begin using the following exercise. This exercise can be used throughout your day.

Exercise 5: Mindfulness

Begin by taking three deep breaths. Allow any thoughts you have to come and go.

Breathe normally now.

Let your focus settle on your breathing.

Feel the rise and fall of your chest as you breathe in and out.

Feel the air as it enters your lungs.

Allow any stress you have to exit with the air as you exhale.

Continue to breathe normally.

Now bring your attention to your heartbeat.

Allow the rhythm to slow with your breath.

As you continue to breathe normally, move your attention around your body.

Allow your muscles to relax. Let any tension leave your body as you exhale.

Now allow your attention to focus on the things around you—the smells, sights, and sounds. Don't analyze anything; just accept it for what it is.

Bring your attention back to your breathing. Feel your chest rise and fall.

Now take three deep breaths.

If it will benefit you, you can record this and use it to guide yourself until you become familiar with the exercise.

"The most powerful affirmations are those you say out loud when you are alone in front of the mirror."

—Unknown

Chapter 11

Words Matter—Affirmations

When attempting to change your beliefs, or anything really, words do matter. The way you speak to yourself becomes ingrained. And is likely the reason you're seeking to change your beliefs now.

Throughout your life there have probably been many times that the stories you told yourself, the things you said that only you could hear, were undeniably negative. Things like "I'm not good enough," "I will never have enough money," or even a truly simple one such as "I can't do that."

This is where affirmations come in. You'll be writing affirmations to help you in your journey to change the way you think about yourself. Affirmations will be something in your arsenal to combat the negative thoughts that you repeat on a daily basis.

I'm sure you've heard of affirmations before, since they seem to be everywhere. Let's take a look at what they are. They are simply positive statements that you can use to challenge the negative thoughts that are keeping you from change. Affirmations are something that can be repeated daily. They can aid you in being more resilient when dealing with stressful situations.

Positive affirmations need repetition in order for them to be successful. The negative thoughts (which are really affirmations too) running through your head took time to build up. This is true for positive affirmations as well. They need daily repetition in order for them to sink into your subconscious.

Affirmations have been scientifically proven. There is a psychological theory behind them not just popular belief. Positive affirmations require you to practice them regularly in order for them to become lasting and to make the changes that you wish to see.

Affirmations should be written down, and then verbally repeated two to three times a day, such as when you wake up in the morning and before you go to bed at night. Repetition is the key to success with affirmations (and many other things).

They are not a quick fix. They require patience and consistency. You should use the present tense when writing your affirmations; don't focus on the past. They should also be something that you believe. They should be written in terms that your subconscious will accept, not an outlandish statement... such as "Money flows freely to me" instead of "I will win a hundred million dollars in the lottery."

Affirmations should be simple and memorable. If you create a huge, complex sentence as an affirmation, you will be less likely to remember it or use it. If you make them too long, you run the risk of turning your affirmations into a chore.

Beginning your day with affirmations will allow you to set the tone for your day. It will put your thoughts into alignment with what you wish to achieve. A simple affirmation such as "Today will be a good day" will allow your mind to see the positive around you instead of focusing on the negative.

Exercise 6: Affirmations

In this exercise, you will need your responses from Exercise 3.

Take a clean sheet of paper and divide it into four with a line down the center, horizontally and vertically.

In each of the sections, you will break down your previous answers into their simplest form. You may need to write this several times. If your affirmations are too long, don't give up. Just refine them until you get them down to one short sentence.

Do this for each of the sections from Exercise 3. On the upper left will be your new belief.

On the upper right will be the thoughts surrounding your new belief. The lower left will be the emotions tied to your new belief, and the lower right will be the actions you take to form your new belief.

Take your time; there is no need to rush through this. Put some serious thought into the words you use. The words you use should be words you would say. If you speak straightforwardly and to the point, that is how your affirmations should be written. If you use elaborate words when you speak, then write your affirmations as such.

Once you have your affirmations for all four squares written, try to condense them even further down. Work to combine the four squares into as few sentences as possible. If you can't reduce them further, that's fine. But if you can, it will make them easier to remember and use.

After you have reduced your affirmations as much as possible, take a clean sheet of paper and write them down. Do this in your own handwriting. Say the words as you write them. Believe what you are writing. Allow yourself to absorb the words and feel them radiate throughout your whole being.

Now that you have your affirmations written, it's time to put them to use. You should say your affirmations out loud at least two or three times a day: once in the morning, right after you wake up, and once just before you go to sleep. If at all possible, you should say them a third time in the middle of the day. I know that may be difficult if you work and there are people around. In that case, say them to yourself. Or say them while you are at lunch. The more you repeat them, the better.

In the morning, when you wake up, stand in front of a mirror, look yourself in the eyes, and say your affirmations out loud. Repeat them three times. Keep eye contact with yourself. When you first do this, it will feel uncomfortable. Don't let that distract you. Say your affirmations firmly. Say them with conviction. Believe them!

At midday, repeat your affirmations. Speak them as a statement; know they are true. Even if you need to say these silently, speak them as the truth. Know that the changes you seek are yours for the taking.

In the evening, when you are getting ready for bed, you can do your affirmations in one of two ways. You can stand in front of the mirror (as you did in the morning) and repeat your affirmations. Or you can get into bed, relax, and state your affirmations just before turning off the lights to go to sleep. Regardless of which option you choose, say your affirmations as statements. Don't be wishy-washy or half-hearted. Repeat them, knowing that they will guide the changes you wish to make. Repeat your affirmations three times, imagining how your life will be better with the changes you desire being completed.

"Every day, in every way, I am getting better and better."

—Émile Coué

Chapter 12

Self-Hypnosis

Now that you have all the pieces in place, it's time to bring them all together. We will use your breathing and your mindfulness and add to that your new beliefs and your affirmations.

I hope that you have completed all the exercises up until this point. Don't skip any of them as they will build upon each other. If you were tempted to skip ahead, I encourage you to go back and do the exercises in the sequences they were presented, because in this chapter we will be using self-hypnosis to pull all the practices and information from the previous chapters into one cohesive process.

Self-hypnosis is the last practice in this process. As you may have noticed up until this point, we have looked at various other forms to begin to allow your mind to accept the changes you desire. Each of the practices and exercises will allow the self-hypnosis to be more easily accepted by your subconscious.

Whether you are utilizing a hypnotist or you are in the comfort of your home doing it yourself, hypnosis is not magic. Hypnosis does require that you suspend your doubts and disbeliefs. If you believe that the changes you desire can be reached, then you will achieve them.

The only thing holding you back is your beliefs. That is not something that should scare you away from making changes. In fact, if you look at it like this, I believe it will encourage you to step forward and create a better life. **The beliefs you now hold were created by you.** Therefore, you already know that you can create new beliefs. You already know that your subconscious is an incredible asset, and if you direct it and stay consistent, your new beliefs are yours for the taking.

There are a couple of other things you should be aware of:

The first is that other people will not always support you. This is due to the simple fact that it makes them feel like they are not trying to better themselves. We all have those people in our lives. If you have someone in your life that is going to naysay you on your journey, do your best to avoid them. You will also find that as you change your beliefs, a new group of people will come into your life. People who are changing themselves and who will support you.

And the second, depending on what you are trying to change, is the outside world. Specifically, the news and media. If you are changing your beliefs about stress or anxiety, the best advice I can give you is to turn off the TV and stay off social media, at least for a short time. Both of those tend to push the negative. You can cut them out or at least limit your time spent with them. I assure you that the woes of the world will still be there a week or month from now.

About eight years ago, I stopped watching the news. I found that every time I watched it, I felt disappointed and disillusioned afterward. It was one of the best things I've done. My spirit lifted and I didn't want to hide in my house and never come out. I still get information, but I've broken it down into bite-size amounts instead of the hour-long fearmongering that seems to be on every news channel. All I'm saying is that if I can do it, so can you.

Please don't take any of the above as a reason to give up. I think that one of the biggest issues with the self-help/motivational market is that it doesn't always give you all the information. I assume that's so you'll go back and buy more. I gave you that information because I believe that the better informed you are, the more likely you are to succeed in making your changes permanent.

You should also be aware that this will likely not be a one-and-done. I would suggest at least practicing your chosen exercises three times. Once a week is recommended. This is simply the best approach to making sure that the changes you seek are reinforced in your subconscious. Just like your breathing exercises, your mindfulness exercises, and your affirmations, your self-hypnosis exercise needs to be repeated to achieve your goals.

At this point, you should have a solid idea of what you want to change. The previous exercises should have distilled your new beliefs into a small consumable bite-size. The breathing and mindfulness exercises will allow you to relax and ease into the self-hypnosis exercise in this chapter.

Before delving into the exercise, I want to remind you that you are in control. You have a say in how effective this exercise turns out. Hypnosis, whether self-induced or guided by a professional, relies on you wanting to be hypnotized. Begin the exercise by telling yourself that you want to be hypnotized so that you can make the changes to better yourself.

Now is the time that you have been preparing for. Now is the time for you to speak directly to your subconscious and tell it how much you are looking forward to making these changes. Now is that time to become the you that you want to be.

Let's begin…

Exercise 7: Self-Hypnosis

Find a comfortable spot where you will not be disturbed. You can lie down on a bed or on the floor. Or sit comfortably in a chair.

I want you to find a spot on the wall in front of you. It could be a discoloration in the paint or wallpaper. Or maybe the corner of a picture frame. Or simply a blemish on the wall.

Focus all of your attention on that spot. Allow everything around it to fade. Keep your attention on that spot.

In a moment, not yet, I'm going to count from three to one. On one, not before, you will close your eyes. Then I will count from one to three and you will open your eyes. We will do this three times. When you open your eyes, look only at the spot on the wall.

We will begin now…

3…2…1 Close your eyes. Allow your mind to see the spot on the wall, all its detail, just as if you were still looking at it. Isn't it amazing what your mind can see?

1…2…3 Open your eyes, focus on the spot. The edges around the spot are faded and blurry.

3…2…1 Close your eyes. Allow your mind's eye to begin to make the spot fuzzy and out of focus.

1…2…3 Open your eyes. The spot will begin to look out of focus, just like your mind imagined it.

3…2…1 Close your eyes. Allow your mind to let the spot move further and further away, until it completely dissolves and is gone.

Keep your eyes closed now.

Take a deep breath in. Feel it enter your nose and travel to your lungs, expanding your chest. Now, release that breath and feel any stress or discomfort leaving your body.

Take another deep breath in, feeling the oxygen rushing through your body. Release that breath and allow yourself to relax.

And once more: Take a deep breath in, allowing your mind to relax. And release that breath, allowing your body to completely let go.

Breathe normally now. Feel the air flow through your nose. Feel your lungs expand and contract. Feel the blood as it carries the oxygen throughout your body. Breathe normally and continue to relax.

I want you to place your focus on the top of your head, right at the crown. I want you to imagine a warm, bright light shining down on the top of your head. Feel the muscles in your scalp relax. As the light continues to radiate downward, allow the tension in your forehead to release. Feel the muscles of your jaw loosen.

As the light hits your neck and shoulders, feel the muscles relaxing, releasing any tension. As the light continues to envelop you, feel your chest and abdomen letting go of any stress you have there. Feel your upper and lower arms releasing tension. Allow your hands to go limp with comfort. As the light continues downward, feel any tension or stress in your hips and thighs just fade away. Feel your knees, shins, and calves relax.

And finally, as the light reaches your feet, feel your ankles and toes grow relaxed and heavy. Feel your entire body and mind completely relaxed and at ease.

Continue to breathe normally. Hold on to your relaxation and bring your attention to your breath. Feel the rise and fall of your chest. Feel the air fill your lungs and then as they empty with your exhale. Pay attention to each breath, in and out, in and out. Feel a sense of calm. Allow that calm to penetrate every molecule of your being. Breathe in and out, in and out. Now bring your focus to your heartbeat. Allow it to be the only thing you hear. Breathe in and out. Feel the blood flow with each pump of your heart. Breathe in and out. Continue to breathe. Continue to relax.

Now I want you to bring your attention to the sounds around you. Don't analyze them, just accept them as they are. Hear the hum of any machinery in the room. Perhaps you hear birds or crickets or maybe even frogs. Accept them for what they are, nothing more. Take a moment and just revel in all the sounds surrounding you. Feel the air in the room. Perhaps it's cool and crisp, or maybe it's warm and inviting. Feel the way it touches your skin. Just be present in this moment. Breathe, relax, and know you are here and now.

Now, bring your attention to your mind. Allow yourself to travel to that place in your mind where your feelings and emotions dwell. This is the place where your beliefs reside. This is where you will introduce the changes you wish to make. Picture this as a room. And in the center of this room is a large, comfortable reclining chair. Walk to that chair and sit down. Reach down and pull the lever; the footrest rises up to meet your feet. Allow yourself to relax and get comfortable. Continue breathing normally. Your whole body is relaxed as if you were suspended in midair.

I want you to take a deep breath now. Breathe in and exhale. And again, breathe in and release it. Once more, take a deep breath in and exhale out.

You are now going to state the new belief you want to have. Do that now. State your new belief (use the worksheet from Exercise 3). Feel that belief fill the room. Feel it permeate the walls. Feel it take up all the space in your room.

Continue breathing normally.

Now you are going to state the emotions you want attached to this new belief. State it as "This belief will make me feel ……………….." insert your emotion (use the worksheet from Exercise 3). Proudly proclaim it.

Allow your belief and emotion to become intertwined. Continue to breathe normally and remain relaxed.

Sit in your room for a moment. Allow your subconscious to fully accept your new belief and the emotions behind it. Allow the belief to fully fill the room.

(Allow 30 seconds of silence here)

Now, put the footrest down and stand up. Know that your belief has been delivered to your subconscious.

I want you to leave your room now. Bring your attention to your breathing. Feel the air filling your lungs. Hear your heartbeat as it pumps blood through your veins. Allow yourself to come back to the here and now. Continue breathing normally.

In a moment, not yet, but in a moment, I will count from 1 to 3. When I reach 3, you will open your eyes.

1… Each day you will take the steps necessary to bring your desired changes into being.

2… As your energy begins to rise, you know that your changes have been processed by your subconscious.

3… Open your eyes feeling relaxed, rejuvenated, and ready to conquer your dreams.

I suggest that you record this exercise so that you can concentrate on the process and allow yourself to accept the hypnosis. There are two places that you will need your responses from the worksheet from Exercise 3.

"Repetition is the mother of learning, the father of action, which makes it the architect of accomplishment."

—Zig Ziglar

Chapter 13

Repetition

Look at you! Doing the work required to make the changes you seek. Putting forth the effort to change your life. Confronting and modifying the beliefs that have held you back.

Now, it's time for the secret sauce that will solidify your goals—**REPETITION.**

Repetition is the key to being successful. Not only in the current endeavor you are embarking upon but in most everything you do. It's the secret to learning. Think of it like this: The beliefs that you want to change were not created overnight. They took time to become instilled in your subconscious and, in turn, dictate the actions of your life—your choices and your views. And those thoughts, emotions, and actions were created by repetition.

Your mind is always trying to provide you with validation of what you think. And the validation of those thoughts trigger emotions. And those emotions are what cause the actions you take.

The quest (yes, it's a quest, move over Frodo!) you have accepted is to change those thoughts so that your mind can validate uplifting and positive feedback. Once your mind has accepted this new challenge, your life will never be the same.

Imagine waking up in the morning and thinking *What a wonderful day today is going to be* instead of dreading the day. Perhaps you'll have the confidence to speak up when you have something to say. Knowing that you can achieve any goals you've set for yourself.

People are creatures of habit. Which is why it seems impossible to change deep-seated beliefs. It feels easier to remain tethered to something that you know is not good for you. But not **YOU**! You have chosen to make changes. You have chosen to improve yourself.

Repetition reinforces new information. That's the importance of repetition. It solidifies learning. And learning is what you are doing now. You are learning that your beliefs can be changed. You are learning that no matter your past, you can change your future.

Science has proven that repetition physically changes the communication of your brain.

You are creating new neural pathways. Imagine your neural pathways as a walkway going through a treed grove. It is sunny, and the trees are green and lush. There's a slight, comfortable breeze. The birds are chirping and singing. You feel fantastic. Doesn't that sound wonderful? That is a new neural path. That is so much better than the old neural pathway that was cold, dark, and uninviting. Don't you agree?

When you stimulate your brain with repetition, information is better remembered and retained for a longer time. That is a benefit since you are creating new beliefs. Repetition optimizes new learning.

Through repetition, things become more familiar. And that is precisely what you want when changing your beliefs. You want your new beliefs to become familiar, so that your responses to situations are changed for the better.

Another thing that science has proven is that people are more likely to believe something is true the more they hear it. The more it is stated, whether audibly or visually, the more it is retained and believed. Even if you know the information is wrong. This is how you end up with belief systems that do harm.

It's time to use that information to your advantage. Your breathing practice, your mindfulness practice, and your affirmations will be your repetition. By daily repeating your affirmations and being present in your life, you will change your neural pathways. And that will change your life.

Change takes time. Just like the belief system you are changing took time to create, replacing it with a new belief will take time. I wish I could tell you that the changes you wish to make will be instantaneous, but that would be a lie. It takes persistence and repetition to achieve those goals. I think the self-help industry fools people into believing that things will happen overnight. I am telling you this because I want you to succeed! And I know that you can!

"You can have anything you want if you are willing to give up the belief that you can't have it."

—Dr. Robert Anthony

Chapter 14

A Realistic Timetable

I don't want you to think that I am going to give you information and simply say, "Good luck." I want you to be aware that your goals are within reach and that you can do this. I also want to give you a timeline. This is a basic timeline: You may find you need more time in certain areas to complete the exercises.

I want you to be armed with knowledge so that you don't give up before you get started. This is by no means a magic overnight process. When you truly want to change, there will be no stopping you. Follow the exercises. Be kind to yourself. And above all—BELIEVE IN YOURSELF!

Exercise 1: Acknowledging the Belief

This may be the hardest one to complete. It requires you to be honest with yourself. Take the time and really examine your beliefs. Give yourself 1–2 days to complete this.

Exercises 2 and 3: Writing and Rewriting Your Beliefs

This is where you will decide on the one belief you want to change. Then you will write the new belief you want to create. These two exercises should take 1–2 days.

Exercise 4: Breathing Practice

Once you begin this practice, it will be done daily. Do it at least twice a day. Once in the morning and once in the evening. It will help you regulate your stress and calm your heart rate. You can do this throughout your day if you find yourself becoming overly stressed or simply need a break.

Exercise 5: Mindfulness

This will keep you present and in the moment. It will relax you and allow you to see things for what they are instead of the multitude of what-ifs. This is a daily practice. Do it at least twice a day. Once in the morning and once in the evening. This can be done throughout your day if needed to ground you.

Exercise 6: Affirmations

This exercise should take 1–2 days: the first day to write your initial affirmations and the second to revise and condense them into their simplest form.

Exercise 7: Self-Hypnosis

This exercise should be done once a week for three weeks. You can use it after that if you feel it's necessary as a refresher. Your breathing, mindfulness, and affirmations will fill the time in between using the self-hypnosis.

It takes twenty-one days to create a new habit. And approximately ninety days for that habit to become permanent. Practice the exercises diligently and you will see the changes you seek.

You are capable of change. You are worthy of change. Believe in yourself and you will accomplish the changes you desire.

"Yesterday is gone. Tomorrow has not yet come.
We have only today. Let us begin."

—Mother Teresa

Chapter 15

A Final Thought

Each section of this book will step you closer to your goal until you complete it. Each exercise will give you the clarity you need to move forward. Each exercise builds on the one before it, so don't skip any of them. Let's take a look back at what you have learned.

- Breaking down your beliefs and creating new ones is your roadmap.

- The PN4 breathing exercise will allow you to regulate your breathing and heart rate. This will allow you to relax and aid in releasing negative feelings.

- The mindfulness exercise allows you to be present and access (and inspect) your feelings without being entangled in them.

- Your affirmations are your road signs. They will keep you on track and progressing forward. Saying them daily will keep you on the path to your desired changes.

- The self-hypnosis exercise will allow you to speak directly to your subconscious mind. This will allow your feelings and emotions to align with your desired changes.

- Repetition will develop the roadway (neurological pathways) for future changes to easily travel.

You are now armed with the knowledge and processes to begin your transformation. Throughout these pages, you have learned how to go about making the changes to your belief system to ultimately improve yourself and your life.

I will repeat this once again, this process is not an overnight endeavor. It will take time and commitment on your part. When you follow the path laid out, you will make the changes you seek. After all…. "anything worth doing is worth doing right."—Hunter S. Thompson

At the beginning of this book, I asked you to write down the beliefs you wished to change. If you came up with more than one, I strongly encourage you to focus on one at a time. Go through the process for each belief you want to change. Yes, this will take time. However, by giving each one attention, your success in changing them will vastly increase. If you try to tackle more than one at a time, you may get discouraged and give up before you get started.

This book has provided you with the knowledge to achieve your goal of change. Now it is time to take action and put the principles into practice. Knowledge without action is simply wishful thinking. You must take the first step.

There are a lot of books (and videos and tutorials) out there that share good information. It has been my experience that they do not share all the information. They each seem to provide an incomplete overview of how to make lasting changes. That is the reason I wrote this book. I believe that if you have all the information, making changes to your belief system can be achieved.

I also believe that when setting out to make changes to your beliefs, padding and fluff is not needed (or desired, in most cases). Therefore, I have written this book with that in mind. There is nothing here to distract you from your goals.

The information in this book will guide you in making changes to what you believe to be true. It will help you change the beliefs that you now have in place that no longer serve you. And this information will help you to dissolve and remove beliefs that are causing you pain and keeping you in a repetitive cycle.

However, the most important part of this equation is **YOU**. Your desire to change the belief system that is holding you back. The desire to change your beliefs to create a better life. This all starts with YOU. You must want to change. You must devote the time and energy to changing. And YOU must believe that YOU can change.

This is where people get hung up. They think that they can't change. Or they are simply unwilling to try. I believe that you are ready to change, or why would you have purchased this book?

I have unyielding faith that you can make the changes you desire. Because I have been where you are now. I have procrastinated and put things off. I have worried about what others may think of me. I have had the overwhelming feelings of "something new." In the end, they were just excuses for me not to try. Taking that first step was the hardest, but it was all well worth the effort and time.

I know if you take the time and follow the process in this book, you will reach your goal of change. I know that you can improve your life. I know that the things holding you back can be overcome. I know that you can achieve the things that you desire.

I KNOW YOU CAN DO THIS! BECAUSE I BELIEVE IN YOU! NOW IS THE TIME TO BELIEVE IN YOURSELF!

Acknowledgments

I would like to thank the people who have helped me complete this book:

My family for showing me that even the ones with the best intentions help to build the walls of my beliefs—both good and bad.

My friends for their words of encouragement, whether genuine or not. And those who believed in me when I couldn't find the courage to believe in myself.

I would also like to thank Jason Linnett, Dr. Richard Nongard, and Mel Robbins for showing me that what I was teaching others was all part of the same thought process. For making me realize that what I had to say was indeed worthy of a book. And for the needed kick in the ass to achieve my goals.

Thank you all for your contributions to helping me achieve what I set out to do.

And most of all, I would like to thank you—for purchasing this book and making the decision to change your beliefs and change yourself. I look forward to meeting the person you've set out to become.

Made in the USA
Columbia, SC
10 June 2025